READING POWER

European Colonies in the Americas

Portuguese Colonies in the Americas

Lewis K. Parker

The Rosen Publishing Group's
PowerKids Press™
New York

Published in 2003 by The Rosen Publishing Group, Inc.
29 East 21st Street, New York, NY 10010

First Edition

Book Design: Erica Clendening

Photo Credits: Cover, pp. 8–9, 12–13, 18 © Culver Pictures; pp. 4, 16 Erica Clendening; p. 5 (top) © Corbis; p. 5 (bottom) © The Pierpoint Morgan Library, Art Resource, NY; p. 6 © Giraudon/Art Resource, NY; p. 7 © Nigel Smith/Earth Scenes; pp. 11, 17 © Bettmann/Corbis; p. 13 (inset) © Pablo Corral V/Corbis; p. 14 © Charles O'Rearl/Corbis; p. 15 © Image Select/Art Resource, NY; p. 19 © Reunion des Musees Nationaux/Art Resource, NY; p. 20–21 © Daniel Geller/Corbis

Library of Congress Cataloging-in-Publication Data

Parker, Lewis K.
Portuguese colonies in the Americas / Lewis K. Parker.
 p. cm. — (European colonies in the Americas)
Includes bibliographical references and index.
Summary: Describes the establishment of a Portuguese colony in Brazil in the sixteenth century, the problems with the Dutch and French, the activities of the Portuguese colonists, their interaction with the native inhabitants, and the eventual fate of Brazil.
ISBN 0-8239-6474-4 (library binding)
1. Portuguese—Brazil—History—Juvenile literature. 2. Brazil—History—To 1822—Juvenile literature. 3. Portugal—History—Juvenile literature. [1. Portugal—Colonies—Brazil. 2. Portuguese—Brazil—History. 3. Brazil—History—To 1822.] I. Title.
CURR F2659.P8 P37 2003
981'.03—dc21

2002002936

Contents

Settling Brazil

In 1500, Portugal's king sent Pedro Alvarez Cabral to India to trade. However, storms forced Cabral's ships off course. Instead, Cabral landed on the coast of Brazil on April 22, 1500. Cabral claimed the land for Portugal.

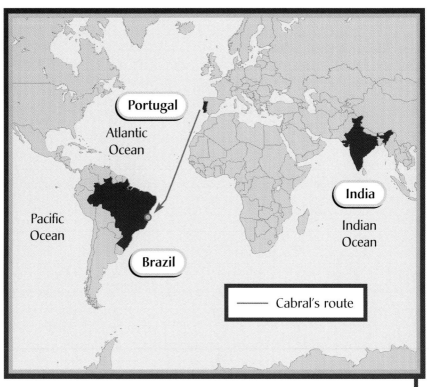

Cabral landed about 10,000 miles away from India.

Pedro Alvarez Cabral

Cabral took thirteen ships when he set sail for India. Cabral lost several of his ships on his trip.

The first Portuguese colony in Brazil was started in 1530. The earliest Portuguese settlements were trading forts.

Many settlers left for Brazil on ships that sailed from Lisbon, Portugal.

Soon, Portugal's government divided Brazil into 15 parts. Each part was controlled by a rich Portuguese family.

The Fact Box

Brazil got its name from the brazilwood tree.

Brazil's native people cut logs of brazilwood. The logs were traded to Portuguese settlers for pots, knives, axes, and other goods made in Europe. The wood of this tree was used to make red or purple dye. Brazilwood was also used to make violin bows.

7

Many Portuguese people believed their church was very important. They wanted the native people in Brazil to share their religious beliefs.

In 1549, people from Portugal came to set up a church in Brazil. They taught the native people about their beliefs.

Some of the Portuguese Settlements in Brazil	
Name	Year Settled
Olinda	1537
Salvador	1549
São Paulo	1554
Minas Gerais	1720

Tomé de Sousa (seated and pointing) founded the Brazilian city of Salvador in 1549.

Problems with the Dutch and the French

Other countries wanted control of Brazil. In 1555, the French started a settlement along the shores of Rio de Janeiro (ree-OH DAY zhuh-NEHR-oh) Bay. The Portuguese army forced the French out of Brazil in 1567.

Then, in 1630, the Dutch took over most of Portugal's land in northeastern Brazil. In 1654, Portuguese colonists took back this land from the Dutch.

Maurice of Nassau was the governor of the Dutch colony in Brazil. He helped the colony grow, and he treated the Portuguese colonists well. However, many other Dutch people wanted to make the Portuguese pay high taxes. Maurice of Nassau did not want to do this. He quit his job in 1644 when the Dutch government did not give him the money he needed to run the colony. The next year, Portuguese colonists began to fight to get back their land from the Dutch.

Plantations and Mines

The Portuguese settlers set up plantations to grow sugarcane. The sugar made from these plants was sent to Europe to be sold. The Portuguese forced the native people of Brazil to work on the plantations.

Plantation workers in Brazil

Many natives died from being badly treated by the Portuguese. Many of them also died from European illnesses caught from the Portuguese.

Sugarcane

African people were brought to Brazil to work on the plantations as slaves. When the Portuguese discovered gold and diamonds in Brazil in the 1690s and early 1700s, the slaves were put to work in the mines. The slaves dug for the diamonds and gold. Then, the gold and diamonds were sent back to Portugal.

Portugal became very rich from selling sugar, gold, and diamonds (pictured).

Slaves cleaning diamonds in Brazil

15

By the late 1780s, many settlers in Brazil wanted to be free of Portugal's control. They had heard about the way the people of the United States had forced the English to leave America. In 1789, a group of settlers tried to overthrow the Portuguese government in Brazil. They failed to win their independence.

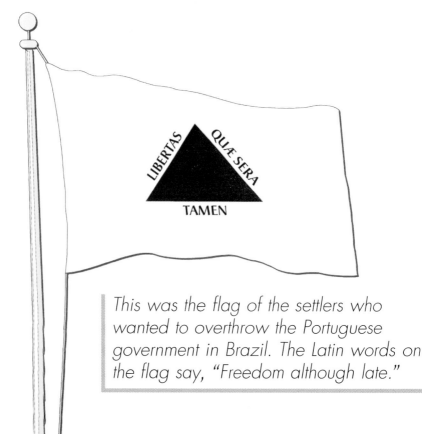

This was the flag of the settlers who wanted to overthrow the Portuguese government in Brazil. The Latin words on the flag say, "Freedom although late."

Thomas Jefferson was one of the people who helped Americans win their independence from England. The people trying to overthrow the Portuguese government asked Thomas Jefferson for help. Jefferson asked the U.S. government to help them, but it did not.

Brazil Gains Independence

In 1807, Napolean Bonaparte, the ruler of France, took over Portugal. Prince John of Portugal escaped to Brazil. There, he set up his kingdom, which lasted until 1821. Then, Prince John returned to Portugal and left his son, Pedro, as ruler of Brazil. In 1822, Pedro freed Brazil from Portugal's rule.

Pedro

Napolean Bonaparte

Brazil Today

Today, Brazil is the fifth-largest country in the world. Over 175 million people live there. Portuguese is the official language of Brazil. Portugal's colonies have left a lasting mark on life in Brazil.

Brazil is the only country in South America that speaks the Portuguese language.

Time Line _____

1500	Pedro Alvarez Cabral finds Brazil and claims it for Portugal.
1530	The first Portuguese colony in Brazil is set up.
1549	People from Portugal set up a church in Brazil.
1560s	African people are brought to Brazil to work as slaves.
1690s–early 1700s	Gold and diamonds are discovered in Brazil.
1807	Prince John of Portugal rules Brazil.
1821	Prince John's son, Pedro, rules Brazil.
1822	Pedro makes Brazil free from Portugal's rule.

Glossary

colony (**kahl**-uh-nee) a faraway land that belongs to or is under the control of a nation

course (**kors**) the direction of travel of a ship

divided (duh-**vyd**-uhd) when something is broken up into different parts

Europe (**yur**-uhp) one of the seven continents where England, France, and Spain are found

independence (ihn-dih-**pehn**-duhns) freedom from being ruled by another

kingdom (**kihng**-duhm) a country that is ruled by a king or queen

plantations (plan-**tay**-shuhnz) large farms where usually only one crop is grown

religious (rih-**lihj**-uhs) having to do with a god or a system of faith

settlements (**seht**-l-muhnts) places where people come to live

settlers (**seht**-luhrz) people who come to stay in a new country or place

slaves (**slayvz**) people who are owned by other people and forced to do work

trading forts (**trayd**-ihng **forts**) strong buildings or places that can be easily guarded and that are used as rest stops for travelers and stores for trading goods

Resources

Books

Vasco da Gama and the Portuguese Explorers
by Jim Gallagher
Chelsea House Publishers (2000)

Brazil
by Ann Heinrichs
Children's Press (1997)

Web Sites

Due to the changing nature of Internet links, PowerKids
Press has developed an online list of Web sites related
to the subjects of this book. This site is updated regularly.
Please use this link to access the list:

http://www.powerkidslinks.com/euca/por/

Index

Word Count: 431

Note to Librarians, Teachers, and Parents

If reading is a challenge, Reading Power is a solution! Reading Power is perfect for readers who want high-interest subject matter at an accessible reading level. These fact-filled, photo-illustrated books are designed for readers who want straightforward vocabulary, engaging topics, and a manageable reading experience. With clear picture/text correspondence, leveled Reading Power books put the reader in charge. Now readers have the power to get the information they want and the skills they need in a user-friendly format.